Born and educated in the North of England, Gwenneth Scott began teaching Ceramics, Art and English, first in Worcestershire and then in Gloucestershire where she settled with her husband and family.

The Cotswolds are a little bit of heaven that she counts herself lucky to have found.

Never one to accept the wasteful 'throw away' culture she promotes a more sustainable and eclectic lifestyle that is more affordable, more fun and contributes to the fight against global warming.

To my family – you are appreciated

Gwenneth Scott

CAN I AFFORD IT?
YES, I CAN.
WHY CAN I AFFORD IT?
BECAUSE...

AUSTIN MACAULEY PUBLISHERS™

LONDON • CAMBRIDGE • NEW YORK • SHARJAH

A CIP catalogue record for this title is available from the British Library.

ISBN 9781398464520 (Paperback)
ISBN 9781398464537 (ePub e-book)

www.austinmacauley.co.uk

First Published 2024
Austin Macauley Publishers Ltd®
1 Canada Square
Canary Wharf
London
E14 5AA

With thanks to my publishers Austin Macauley.

Can I afford it? Yes, I can. Why can I afford it? Because it was sold at a fraction of its original price. Where did I find it? In a charity shop. 'Oh no, you didn't.' 'Oh yes, I did.' Would you like to see some of my other purchases? I bet you would.

I have a wardrobe full of expensive clothes. How is this possible? Because of how I shop and where I shop. I buy only good quality and I am prepared to 'personalise' clothes if necessary. I wear them, I tire of them, I discard them. No, I don't, certainly not, I keep them. I take them out of my wardrobe and I 'box' them. Eventually, they will become vintage garments and be even more desirable.

My other purchases from charity shops include books, lamps, crockery, crystal glasses, casserole dishes, pots and pans, fashion accessories, shoes and objets d'art as well as several pieces of furniture. Welcome to my world.

I would be delighted to give you a glimpse of some of my purchases past and present. Show you some of my old favourites that were replaced by something better. They suffered the indignity of exiting the wardrobe and entering the realm of the plastic boxes where conditions are cramped and outings are few. I may even give some former favourites, now banished to the boxes, another twirl, another opportunity to impress.

Clothes are superficial and not to be taken too seriously or have too much money lavished on them. Perhaps that is true and yet I know what an evaluative society we live in and how influential clothes can be in our lives and in our careers. Visual literacy is a very sophisticated art form and what we wear is indicative of who we are and the path we have chosen in life so I think clothes need to be taken seriously because they are very influential. If we are to be successful, we need to 'dress to impress'.

If you don't believe me, wear a green cardigan or jumper similar in colour to that worn by students at Cheltenham Ladies College. For maximum impact, wear it in Cheltenham and observe the effects.

It's only an experiment! I'm certainly not suggesting that you pretend to be something that you're not, but, like the old school tie, I am saying that clothes have power. Your appearance will influence how people perceive you. They will make instant value judgements based entirely on those first impressions so the clothes you choose to wear, their cut, their colour and the accessories worn with them are very important.

If you would like to create an attractive home, then you need a successful career. There are clothes that will help you to achieve that ambition for a fraction of the usual price. New, professional, designer label clothes, you just have to find them.

Are smart clothes for the aspiring professional really to be found in a charity shop? Yes, they are. How do I know? Because when I first shopped there, that is what I needed, that is what I found and that is what I bought.

There are several notable names here and in my wardrobe. A jacket by Emporio Armani for example, one by Roberto Chiave, a suit by August Silk, a jacket by Marella, one by Hobbs, one that I saved up for and bought by Toi du Monde as well as several dark and nameless dresses and a very useful black cardigan by John Smedley.

Smart clothes for the aspiring young professional.

If you feel that venturing into a charity shop is demeaning and likely to have a detrimental effect on your career prospects, then explain to your colleagues that you find second-hand books fascinating, particularly first editions. You might, I do, I don't actually have any first editions but I would certainly like some. Phew! Your reputation has been rescued, you have been elevated to a 'book collector' with all the accompanying kudos. This can certainly enhance your career prospects. It will suddenly be perfectly acceptable to frequent as many charity shops as you wish. Your employers will love the commercial aspect. Money speaks with a very loud voice in all walks of life. A rather cynical observation but something to be aware of.

I'm now retired but for many years, I have thoroughly enjoyed the treasure hunt that is the charity shop experience. Why not come and join me?

Who doesn't love a treasure hunt! Who wouldn't rather exchange shopping, with its rather predictable outcomes, for the enthralling prospect of a treasure hunt! Is there really treasure to be found? Yes, there is, and you won't even need a metal detector to find it.

The treasure arrives at various times during the week, lorry loads of it as well as individual donations. It is sifted, sorted and priced in readiness for the weekend rush. The sales assistants prepare the shop on a Friday, strategically positioning the most desirable of the recent arrivals so as to catch the customers' eye on Saturday morning. Obviously, if you can, go on a Friday afternoon, just before the shop closes.

Be brave, cast your inhibitions aside. Saturday mornings or, better still, Friday afternoons, will never be the same again!

I will show you my treasure trove and hope to encourage you to find some treasure of your own but remember you are not the only 'hunter-gatherer' there, there are others. Speed and determination are required if you are to be successful.

My modus operandi is as follows. Glance around, identify and collect possible purchases, examine them, reject some, try some, buy some.

Don't lower your standards. Linen with its reassuring solidity and strength, silk with its beguiling delicacy and vibrant colour, cashmere the epitome of luxury, are all waiting to be found, worn and appreciated again.

If this shop doesn't have any today, another might. If you decide to buy and then wish you hadn't, can you return it and get a refund? Find out, preferably before you make the purchase. Usually, you can.

This coat is one of my most-admired buys. Did it come from a charity shop? No, it didn't, but it was bought in a sale at a significantly reduced price. Look in the high-end shops, just don't buy in them unless you really do find something amazing and irresistible. It's good to have a few of those in your wardrobe.

This skirt is also much admired, did it come from a charity shop? Yes, it did. It's versatile and suitable for the city or the coast. I love it, it's one of my favourite recent acquisitions, it was designed by David Nieper and Google, my research assistant, informs me that the actual design is entitled 'Abstract'.

This is a designer coat, bought at the end of my teaching career. It is from an Italian design collection called Ohdd, sometimes spelt OHDD.

This skirt, acquired quite recently from a charity shop was created by David Nieper and the design itself is called Abstract.

Have I convinced you? I do hope so. A Saturday morning or Friday afternoon treasure hunt is great fun whilst at the same time enabling you to make significant financial savings. Why not try it?

Still not convinced? Ask yourself which you would rather be; a mere shopper or an explorer, a treasure hunter, an eco-warrior? They sound far more exciting, don't they, and you won't need to go to distant lands to become one. You could recreate that whole experience right here in your own locality.

Archaeological digs, fascinating. Yet, that same fascination can be yours; you can replicate the experience and indulge in a bit of virtual reality here on your own high street by venturing into shops which contain objects with stories which, if you wish, you can research. Where did they come from, who owned them, and why are they here?

The interior of one of my favourites resembles a souk in Marrakech, The Grand Bazaar in Istanbul. It's undeniably exotic; a kimono and a sari hang side by side, part of a very eclectic mix. Once inside, you have entered a new and intriguing world far removed from the normality of the street outside. You can step inside, enjoy the experience, and then step out again. If like me, you are an armchair traveller, not terribly keen on scorching heat, deserts or danger but very keen on artefacts, then this is perfect for you. You step inside, Moroccan Market; you step outside, back to reality, but possibly having gained a few new treasures in the process.

This is the interior of a charity shop that has a very eclectic mix of clothes.

This is another charity shop that sells books, clothes and bric-a-brac to raise money but also markets new goods made by people in 'third world' countries enabling them to earn a living and feed their families.

Back on the street outside, your life returns to normal. Or does it? Because there is another shop not far away. Not a charity shop this time but a shop that specialises in recycled vintage clothes. If you step over its threshold, you will be transported back in time to a bygone era of romance, glitz and glamour. Shall we take a look? Will there be sequins? Yes, there will and feathers and fur, faux fur, of course, and velvet, lots of velvet. Hasn't life suddenly become much more interesting?

Finally, one last brief excursion into fantasy land because not far away is yet another charity shop offering yet another unique shopping experience. This one exudes French chic, it epitomises the small, exclusive, eye-wateringly expensive boutique, so summon your inner diva, she's there somewhere, and prepare to be impressed. Some of the clothes, on a good day, are exquisite and the prices are ridiculously low. It represents excellent value for money and is definitely worth a visit.

Do I detect a glimmer of interest? Is a treasure hunting eco-warrior about to spring from that rather conventional persona, clutching a contact-less credit card and ready to bag a bargain? I do hope so.

Perhaps you are a young professional, ambitious, work-orientated, saving for that holiday and a deposit on an apartment. Very occasionally, you may need to 'shop till you drop' to indulge in some serious life-affirming retail therapy in order to reclaim your work-life balance.

You know that deferred gratification makes sense but once in a while, you want some pleasure, right here right now. Retail therapy, self-indulgence on a massive scale, a budget-busting, mood-enhancing extravaganza!

What if you could achieve the same effect but without the financial damage? I'm delighted to tell you that you can! Shrewd purchases and carrier bags are the key. If you wish, just for one brief moment, to stride along the high street with multiple carrier bags on your arm, the visible tangible reward for all your diligence and hard work, you can, but not yet.

First, you must locate and buy some bargains, luxury items, and experience the soothing sensation of owning soft beguiling cashmere or pink pearls. I found some, so could you. Only when your very special luxury purchases with their very special price tags have modified your perception of the very special shops they came from can your retail therapy commence.

They have the bargains and they have the bags, many bearing the name of very expensive and desirable retailers. They have the power to elevate your image but will it cost hundreds of pounds? No, it won't. Not if you make all your transactions, every single one, in those very special shops. I'm sure you know the ones I mean.

Perhaps you are a little older. You have achieved one of your lifetime ambitions, you have bought a house. The euphoria may last for several years, the mortgage a lot longer. There may be very little money left for a car, furniture, and clothes. Then children come along and there is even less.

Is there a solution to this problem? Yes, there is. Let me remind you of those special shops. They don't sell cars but some have everything you need to furnish a home and others have lots of clothes. The savings that you make shopping there will enable you to buy the car that you need.

You may be much older, retired, as I am, living on a small pension, aware of those special shops and the hidden treasure within. You may embark, once again, on the treasure hunt that is the charity shop experience. You have expertise and business acumen, not a lot of money but plenty of time. Will there be treasure there for you? Yes, I think there will.

People are beginning to shop more responsibly. They are considering the air miles involved in the production process and our 'global footprint'. There is a growing awareness of the fragility of our planet, a realisation that its resources are not limitless and a growing determination to be less wasteful.

There are sound ecological reasons to transfer your allegiance to the charity shops. Clothes or furniture of good quality should not be wasted, they deserve to be appreciated, sometimes by more than one owner. It's a win-win situation. You buy at a fraction of the price whilst helping, through the charity, people less fortunate than yourself and, at the same time, help save the planet's precious resources. Isn't that something to be proud of? I think it is.

Some years ago, term ended and the holidays began. I realised that I had prioritised work to such an extent that I had no holiday clothes at all. I had lots of work clothes but I had no tops, jeans, tee-shirts, shorts, beach bags, sandals, or sunhats. Now I have. Now I have a wardrobe full of clothes, drawers full of tops, jumpers, cardigans and cupboards full of china, all as a result of one very important decision, to change where I shop. That single decision has increased my purchasing power and completely changed my life to an extent that I would not have believed possible.

I will show you some of the things that I have been able to buy as a result of that decision. Very few expensive purchases just a continued commitment to charity shops over many years and a gradual accumulation of practical household items as well as the very occasional more exotic purchase. The amount of money I have spent has been very small. It has proved to be a very successful strategy for me so I have no hesitation in recommending it to you. I definitely think it's a strategy worth considering. If you are a person of limited financial means but discriminating taste, this approach to shopping could be perfect for you.

The seasons are very significant in the fashion story. To an extent, they define it. The natural world and the seasonal changes in it determine what clothing is appropriate for the time of year.

The lightweight fabrics suitable for a warm spring or summer day are not suitable for the cold winds of autumn or winter and the colour palette used in each season is a reflection of what the natural world is wearing at the time. I particularly like the russets, ochres and umbers of autumn but each season is different and each range of colours is beautiful.

One of my most recent skirts is in an amazing fabric. It has the luminosity of silk but doesn't crease and is the whitest of whites. I'm delighted with it. I am determined to protect its pristine perfection. Such is my enthusiasm and devotion that I may even modify my diet to aid its longevity. I will not drink red wine or eat sweet and sour sauce whilst wearing it. I will also need to be extremely vigilant. It will need to be protected from all saffron-infused food. Within seconds of a sighting of that I would obviously have to go. You just can't be too careful. My white skirt and I would have left the building!

There are a lot of practical items needed to furnish a home. I've always looked in charity shops first and most of these have been found there.

I have always been a staunch supporter of natural fabrics although I am also intrigued by new hybrid mixes. I am particularly fond of linen in spite of the fact that it creases. I have several linen skirts, sometimes they have needed a very hot wash to shrink them or have had decorative borders unpicked to simplify them. It's always worth the effort because linen is expensive to buy new.

I buy good quality clothes, designer clothes if possible, at charity shop prices. I keep them, eventually owning both quality and quantity, a very satisfactory outcome. Would you like to see them? I bet you would. Here are some of my summer clothes: I wear a lot of brights and a lot of whites in summer.

I have also always had quite a few black clothes in my wardrobe. I wear them throughout the year but especially in winter and I enliven them with bright accessories. Perfect for work, they look smart, professional, and chic and for the evening, that little black dress is hard to beat. Would you like a look? I bet you would.

For a special occasion, most people go and buy a special outfit. That is a very expensive way to do it. Much cheaper to buy a special occasion outfit when you see one you like but before you actually need it. Advance preparation, a very good plan. It will be there in your wardrobe, ready to be worn. It's impossible to predict when you will need a special occasion outfit or what your special occasion will be or when special occasion outfits will appear in the charity shops but they do and they are often impressively special. Be ready!

I look for good quality clothes. If possible, designer clothes.

These are some of my 'very brights'.

Here you have autumn clothes contrasted with summer clothes.

These special occasion designer outfits are sometimes the result of bankruptcy, stock clearances or donations; sometimes several arrive together, sometimes only one. They are very desirable and sell very quickly. You need to trust to luck that you will be in the right place at the right time.

A favourite of mine, bought some years ago, is a navy blue crepe and chiffon trouser suit designed by Jean Muir. I love it and have worn it on many occasions. The jacket has been especially useful. The trousers are very long, giving an impression of elegance. Unfortunately, they need to be worn with very high, perilously high wedges. Now that I'm older, I ask myself, is it worth the risk and my cautious health and safety conscious self replies, probably not.

My other amazing special occasion outfit has never been worn. I decided that it was a Christmas present from my two sons. Did I actually tell them? I'm not sure that I did. It is the most amazing colour; a rich, reassuring cream and the jacket is long and flattering. It is covered in ribbon sewn into intricate patterns, opulent and possibly a little decadent. It is completely different to the pared-down simplicity that I usually prefer. It would need to be worn to a very, very special occasion otherwise instead of admiring glances it might well elicit ridicule and rude remarks such as 'who does she think she is?'

Well, I know who I am, I have no illusions of grandeur, although I do like crystal glasses, designer clothes and chandeliers. I know that I am someone of limited financial means and a vivid imagination, an optimist who believes in making the most of life's opportunities.

There are those who will have difficulty in considering a

visit to a charity shop as an opportunity and find it impossible to think of it as a treasure hunt. I hope that you are not one of them because if you are prepared to make that leap of faith, I am certain that you will not be disappointed. Eventually, you will see things that are of good quality, well worth buying and, importantly, very affordable. Why not come and see?

Over the years, I have bought lots of accessories never paying more than a few pounds for them. Some of them are intentionally bright to add a splash of colour or topical interest.

The fashion industry focuses for a brief moment on one thing before moving on very quickly to the next. It focused on jewellery a few seasons ago and so did I, belts the season before and so did I. Bags had their moment in the spotlight and I focused on bags then scarves had theirs and I concentrated my efforts on them. The fashion industry is notoriously fickle, always wanting something new although if you ignore the ephemeral trends and always buy good quality, those clothes and accessories will last.

The career of a supply teacher is sometimes brief and can be precarious. You enter the classroom and within seconds, the class have made up their minds. Do we like her? No, we don't. Will we co-operate? No, we won't! First impressions, so important! Having survived as a supply teacher at various times during a very long teaching career, I know how important first impressions are.

Some of my 'costume jewellery', attractive but not yet valuable.

Bags and scarves.

An understanding of 'visual literacy', as it is called, is an essential prerequisite for success both personally and professionally. Don't get confused with your stripes. Vertical ones are for work situations. Keep the horizontal ones for holidays.

In one particularly tough teaching environment, I noticed that the psychological power of gold, or to be more accurate the power of gold chains, was very much in evidence. Power dressing! Not fine delicate chains, big brutal heavy ones. They transformed the workforce by establishing some very unorthodox links to nightclub bouncers, Hells Angels, and Rock Chicks, that last one may, I admit, be a link too far. An unconventional approach to discipline but effective. Unfortunately, my dressing up box did not include any heavy metal chains, they're not really my style. I managed to survive without them because it was a mercifully brief stay but had it been longer, it may have been necessary to acquire some myself.

The visible trappings of wealth in the form of real gold jewellery and its power to impress is as undiminished today as it has always been but less valuable accessories can always add interest. Some 'gold' earrings added unexpected interest to one of my evenings. They were big bold pieces of costume jewellery with visual impact. They certainly had that because apparently, the design on them was the logo of the 'Ban the Bomb' movement which was making headline news at the time and not in a good way. Had I noticed? No, I hadn't. Would I have worn them if I had? Probably not.

I now have a large collection of accessories added to gradually over the years. Have I lavished vast amounts of money on them? No, I haven't, they all came from charity shops and cost a few pounds. I have kept the price tags as proof of purchase as I always do. An unusual hobby perhaps, but one that I can recommend. Knowing that the money I spent was also helping those in need and was a way of charitable giving added to the pleasure of my purchases.

If you do decide to visit one or two charity shops, just to have a quick look, remember to expect the unexpected. Winter boots may arrive during a heatwave and summer dresses when it's snowing. You really never know what you will find. This adds a frisson of excitement to the unique challenge that the charity shop experience offers. It is a challenge and who doesn't like a challenge? Perhaps some clothes have been incorrectly sized. Will you notice? Are you an opportunist able to grasp those unexpected treasures? You will need to be quick, observant and adaptable to be successful.

If a lorry load of shoes has just arrived, is it sensible to persist in your plan to look for a pink cardigan? No, it is not, get some shoes. If the shop is overflowing with scarves, do not move them aside to look at the blouses, get a scarf.

One of the most difficult challenges is to find those elusive designer brands. You may have had reservations about going into a charity shop. Exclusive design houses and famous brands share your reluctance, they don't want their creations going into a charity shop either so before that happens, they may remove the label, making your task even harder.

Confronted by a bewildering collection of clothing, it really is a challenge to identify the good, better, and best amongst them but it becomes easier. Once you have had the best, bought the best and worn the best, you won't want anything of inferior quality. If you do want the best, you may need to spend significantly more time and effort finding them.

Occasionally, you may be lucky, as I was recently. Suddenly, there in front of me was a truly beautiful satin dress. It had one vibrant colour merging effortlessly into another. The effect was stunning. I couldn't quite believe my eyes because only a few minutes earlier, in a different shop with very different prices, I had been admiring a lovely and very expensive scarf. I felt my cash card tremble but it needn't have worried, I left the shop. This dress was very similar, just as beautiful and at a very affordable price. Did I buy it? Yes, I did. Of course, I did. Serendipity – it does happen, it could happen to you.

I've always loved linen. I know it creases but my enthusiasm is undiminished. I feel safe in a linen dress and I saw one very recently. A delightful linen dress in the palest of blues. I had just returned from visiting the Cornish coast where I was reminded of the beauty of the colour blue by the great expanse of sea and sky shimmering in a luminous incandescent light. Did I buy the blue dress? Yes, I did.

Shopping in these special shops requires complete concentration. It can be quite an exhausting process, examining, differentiating making the decision to buy or not to buy. Not always one to voluntarily give my brain unnecessary exertion, I have 'stayed the course'. Has it been worth that extra effort? Yes, I can say with absolute unequivocal conviction that it has. You might dip your toe into the water at first but if you fully immerse yourself in the experience, good things will follow.

Take Google with you. To buy or not to buy, that is the

question. Google may help you decide but learn from past experience. I would buy a fine delicate scarf, for example, but would be very unlikely to buy a flimsy dress unless it had a very substantial lining. I once had a gossamer-thin summer dress which disintegrated in the heat. Unfortunately, I was wearing it at the time. It was rather an unnerving experience and not one I wish to repeat any time soon. My disintegrating dress was not, I hasten to add, a charity shop purchase.

Whilst looking in a newly opened charity shop hoping to find a water jug, I saw yet another summer dress. Newly opened shops need to establish their clientele so they are always full of bargains. I could see immediately that it was a 'good buy'; classic style, attractive pattern, fully lined, it would have been expensive. It still had its original label with its original price, it had been very expensive. Did I buy it? Yes, I did. Did I ever find a water jug? Yes, I did, another day in another shop.

I will not buy any more summer dresses for a very long time unless I see an absolutely irresistible one, but you could, there are lots left in the shops for you!

Imperfections, how do you feel about them? Are you sufficiently blasé not to be embarrassed if their imperfections are noticed? I have one or two imperfects. I have a linen blouse with an extra buttonhole. Does it bother me? No, not at all. I have a cardigan with an open weave and attractive colour combinations. I suspected it was too small but bought it anyway. It pulled away in several places almost immediately. I refer to it affectionately as my 'holier than thou' cardigan but if you prefer your treasures pristine and perfect, then that's what you should buy.

Obviously, you will always give the clothes you buy a very thorough wash. A red dress I bought must have missed an important production process because when I washed it, it bled red dye, lots and lots of red dye. Luckily, I hand-washed it so nothing else was damaged. Had I worn it unwashed in the rain, well, that could have been spectacularly embarrassing. Fortunately, that catastrophe was averted.

Fashion embraced the 'distressed denim look' when the economy had a wobble a few years ago and this has made us more tolerant of 'clothes with character'. Be positive. If it has a tear but you like it, negotiate a price reduction, buy it then repair the tear.

This was not an uncommon occurrence until recently. A marketplace mentality prevailed in the charity shops. Today, you are very unlikely to find any imperfect garments because they are so rigorously sorted and only perfect ones are offered for sale. Most of them are new and a significant number are designer brands. What's not to like!

I have gradually added to my jumpers and cardigans over the years. Some I've bought from charity shops, one or two belonged to my mother, a great advocate of the waste not want not philosophy and, a few I have bought new. Then suddenly, last winter, the charity shops in this area were inundated with jumpers and cardigans in every conceivable colour, they were brand new, they were beautiful and they were cashmere! Yes, really, cashmere.

The months leading up to Christmas are often full of opportunities. There is treasure to be found, bargains of all kinds, but last winter I think of as the 'cashmere Christmas'. It was a once-in-a-lifetime opportunity. Did I buy some?

Yes, of course I did. I was reminded of the crystal glass Christmas, the tree decoration Christmas and the Perthshire paperweight summer which were similarly unexpected phenomena.

I can remember several times when 'special occasion' hats have made an appearance. They came quite suddenly and filled the shop. Not modest little hats, these were amazing creations with swirls of net in a symphony of colours. Big and beautiful, they caused a sensation. There was a frenzy of activity, lots of satisfied customers, then, the few remaining hats moved on. Where did they go and where had they come from? No one was saying.

Did I buy one? Of course I did. It's there with my special occasion outfit for my next special occasion. Advance planning, so important!

Small, exquisite 'fascinators' also made a sudden brief appearance. Did I buy one? Yes, I did. My hat, my fascinator and several other more practical hats have been bought gradually over the years. My leather hat was an impulse buy from a charity shop. I'm not intending to go on safari any time soon but if I ever do, I'll have just the right hat to wear.

Hats that keep your hair dry and suitable for my other survival strategy, rambling, are also available. If charity shops have fed my imagination then rambling has fed my soul.

I have felt ramblings mood-enhancing power so often, partly the great outdoors, partly the convivial company and perhaps the effect of those invisible endorphins; it's a truly healing, elemental and restorative experience. The physical exertion, the rain on your face, the wind in your hair, squelching through muddy fields then a long relaxing soak in a warm bath, try it, such a simple remedy but so very effective.

I had several embarrassing moments as a novice rambler. There was my fake fur hat for example. It was never intended for rambling but it was winter and it was cold. Bad idea! The cold day turned into a very wet day and that fur hat absorbed water like a sponge. Nevertheless, I persisted with the rambling because it was definitely more enjoyable than golf.

I had tried golf some years earlier but realised almost immediately that unless they moved those irritating little holes much closer together and made them much bigger, I was doomed to fail. However, I also realised that I did enjoy the walking so rambling seemed the obvious choice of leisure activity. It was the right decision, I absolutely love it.

In an effort to keep embarrassing moments to an absolute minimum, I went to the specialist equipment outdoor pursuits shops and studied what I ought to be wearing, which was waterproof everything. Did I buy anything there? No, I didn't, but at least I knew what I needed. I found all my equipment gradually in charity shops. What I bought is really good quality and only cost a few pounds.

I am now fully equipped for rambling and here are some of the things I have collected. Take a look. I am particularly fond of my walking stick. If it could talk, it could tell you tales from the Tyrol, it's been there and has badges from the area emblazoned down its length. I found it and another one in a charity shop. They were recent arrivals from the auction, unsold and unwanted, I wanted them! Did I buy them? Yes, I did.

Hats, lots of hats and rambling equipment including my rambling sticks.

The one I use has many more badges than the other and has probably walked further. People are always very impressed by my stick but disappointed to discover that I can tell them nothing at all about its travels.

Why not join a rambling club, there are lots of them, get out and explore our glorious countryside? The equipment you need can all be found in charity shops and you will have fun finding it. First, visit the charity shops so that you are able to dress to impress, then, contact a rambling group or perhaps an orienteering group. Give it a go. You'll enjoy it.

Herringbone tweed winter coats are a particular favourite of mine. The pattern reminds me of marking students present on the attendance register I completed each morning as a teacher. I wore a herringbone tweed suit for my interview at Teacher Training College and I have worn several herringbone tweed jackets since.

Now, for winter warmth, I tend to choose light feather-filled coats. They are expensive to buy new but are often available in the charity shops. The more traditional waxed cotton waterproof coats are another favourite of mine. Perfect for walking the dog. I don't have a dog but I do have a waxed cotton coat and a waxed cotton jacket which I keep in readiness for heavy rain.

My 'retirement present' coat is brought out occasionally. The catalogue of the design collection it was part of was given to me as an added incentive to buy although, being a practical person, the fact that it was significantly reduced in price was a more influential factor. I noticed the coat through the shop window, pinioned to the wall as part of a wall display. I had difficulty justifying the price to myself but designating it a retirement present helped.

Winter skirts, I have a few. Black ones, of course, but this tweed skirt is one of my favourites. I got it several years ago, its label is still there and tells me it was designed by Mr & Mrs MacLeod. A more recent favourite winter skirt is by Alex & Co. If you are lucky enough to find a label in the clothes you buy, you can do some research. I've done this several times aided and abetted by my research assistant Google, who confirmed that I had indeed found a bargain. The price differential was significant. Believe me, the opportunities are there, I would encourage you to take them.

Are there genuine bargains to be found? Yes, there are. How do I know? Because I'm sitting on one, drinking my coffee from another and wearing that particularly attractive skirt I mentioned earlier.

Corduroy velvet, it reminds me of ploughed earth and it's perfect for autumn and winter days. Do I have any? Yes, I do. I also love velvet, particularly for evenings; so soft, sumptuous, luxurious, feminine and flattering, it's one of my favourite fabrics. Do I have any in my wardrobe? Yes, I do.

Sequins say Christmas to me, bright lights and sparkling dresses, seasonal festivities. Do I have any? Yes, I do. I have clothes that are covered in sequins and some that have just a scattering but they glint and glimmer and have an undeniable glamour. Not as dazzling as diamonds or gemstones but they sparkle, shine and shimmer, they have a bit of magic about them.

Glamorous sequins and practical denim.

Every few years, there is a denim moment. Do I have any denim? Yes, I do. Would you like to see it? I bet you would.

Perhaps you have decided to take some of your clothes to a charity shop. You have been persuaded to try a 'capsule wardrobe'. Hang on to your possessions is my advice. If you really must be 'on-trend', then create your 'capsule wardrobe' but store your surplus clothes in plastic boxes. A few seasons on, after a few alterations, some of them may find favour again.

I remember when we moved into this house. The garden was full of stones, rocks and boulders. They took a considerable amount of time, effort and energy to move. Soon after this, we designed our garden and decided we would like to create a rockery. Obviously, we would require stones, rocks and boulders. It took considerable time, effort and energy to move them back. Waste not want not comes to mind. Welcome to my world.

Am I materialistic? No, I'm not, but I am practical and I was delighted to see a sign advertising Alterations. Did Sandra with her sewing machine work her magic on some of my purchases? Yes, she did. She took hems up, she let hems down, she took bits out and added bits in. She gave them all a new lease of life. Waste not want not; you know it makes sense.

Personally, I always buy new shoes. Can you find them in charity shops? Yes, you can.

Shoes, lots of charity shop shoes and all brand new.

I once bought some almost new and gorgeous black leather fashion boots. I remember those boots very well. Soon after this, I bought some almost new leather rambling boots. The fashion boots were a disaster and damaged my feet; we are talking extreme, excruciating, memorable, pain! The rambling boots were brilliant and gave me twenty years of excellent service. Don't risk it is my advice, you don't need to. Charity shops get mostly brand-new footwear of all kinds. People don't always realise that. I'm rather particular about shoes but I haven't been disappointed. Here are some of my favourites.

When I first started teaching art and design, no art department was without its shelf of objets d'art. On it was a mix of 'man-made' and 'natural objects'. Proficiency in drawing them was a key component of the syllabus.

The first school I taught in had a glorious collection of birds that the taxidermist had preserved. We drew their feathers, their talons, and appreciated their plumage. Ollie the owl was my favourite and he resided, like the others, in a glass case and peered down at us from a high shelf. We had boxes of shells which were studied and drawn by students year after year. I have a few shells of my own now because of a clearance sale. I love shells, so very beautiful.

We were a traditional art department but not lacking in imagination as was apparent one winter when we had snow, lots of snow. So when life gives you snow, what do you make? Snowmen? Don't be silly, no, you don't. We were an art department, not a nursery school. You make snow sculptures of course. I can't claim the idea but I certainly embraced it and the students were hastily introduced to the sculptures of Henry Moore. No snowmen were created but, working in groups, some large and impressive snow sculptures were and the students loved it.

My own shelf of objet d'art and one of the objects on it.

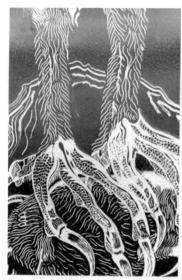

I have no record of the student who did this work but I used it as an example of excellence so thank you that student.

The shells are ones I bought in a clearance sale I find them very beautiful.

As a teacher dedicated to heightening students' appreciation of the natural world and of man-made artefacts, objets d'art hold a special fascination for me and I remember, with regret, the treasures that I couldn't quite afford. The best ones always seemed to appear when I could least afford them. A sizeable 'slice' of crystal came and went. I hesitated too long and it was gone.

I now have my own shelves of objets d'art. Amongst them are a group of Perthshire paperweights. I have always admired Perthshire paperweights. I never expected to own one but one summer, there they were, a breath-taking sight to behold. I was mesmerised. They were on display in the window of a charity shop. A sizeable number had just arrived. Did I buy one? Yes, I did; first one, then another and another.

They stayed long enough for me to buy several. It was an agonising decision choosing which to have. They came in different colour combinations and different sizes, each in its own presentation box lined with white satin. The variation in size was probably the reason they were there but I was delighted with them.

I got to know a couple whose passions were wine and glass paperweights about this time. A room in their house was dedicated entirely to paperweights. It was a stunning sight, quite overwhelming. I was lost for words. My impression was that they had been collected gradually over many years; each one seemed to be unique and each I expect had its own story.

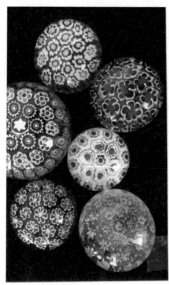

Perthshire paperweights and some beautiful glass found amongst the bric-a-brac in a charity shop and now on my objet d'art shelves.

Each of my objets d'art has its own story. They hold a memory. Most have been bought and some have been given. Some belonged to my parents or my grandmother and a few belonged to an enigmatic aunt on my mother's side of the family who travelled the world. Everybody should have one of those. I never met my great aunt although I do have a photograph, or to be more accurate, half a photograph and an eclectic mix of souvenirs that belonged to her.

There is a fly swatter made from horsehair, essential for travelling in the tropics. A book with an olive wood cover which contains pressed flowers and photographs from the Holy Land. A very decorative Victorian greetings card with moveable parts and romantic messages. There was a bead bag, lace which she had embroidered, a sterling silver thimble in its own case, a tortoise shell hair ornament, several buttons, one made of ivory with a leopard's head incised on it and a small tapestry of a bird that she created from beads and silk threads.

These objects were my first examples of treasure and the fact that I know so little of her life story only adds to their fascination.

I love vintage china, but space on my objets d'art shelves is limited so I have been very selective and chosen only two pretty porcelain cups and saucers as thin as eggshells and completely translucent. Vintage cups, saucers and plates often make an appearance amongst the bric-a-brac in the charity shops, sole survivors of china tea sets from another era.

My first examples of treasure from a great aunt,
including her Victorian greetings card.

More little bits of inspiration that have travelled down the generations bequeathed to me by my great aunt.

In the case of vintage china, I became aware of how it could be used in a different way when I saw the work of Cleo Mussi. Cleo Mussi is a ceramicist specialising in mosaics who lived and worked in this area and probably still does. She produced quirky modern mosaics from a combination of vintage china and tessera made from plain glazed clay tiles. The patterned china adds a rich decorative element. I particularly liked the way she used the handles of the cups to create the ears of her mosaic men, women and children. An original idea with a touch of humour.

Some years ago, I found myself joining one of her studio sessions where she demonstrated her technique. This was a gift from a school where I had worked – thank you that school, you know who you are. We snipped away at china and tiles to create the equivalent of tessera, reassembling them to create our own mini-mosaics. Enjoyable? Yes. Exhausting? Very. It took considerable muscle power to chop that china into pieces. I was enthusiastic but realistic. Would my older students have the physical strength and stamina to make a recycled mosaic? Probably not.

I've had an interest in mosaics since childhood. Ever since one was created by accident. It was a compressed dirt path that turned unexpectedly into a thing of beauty. The soil and rubble used to make it included hundreds of fragments of broken blue and white china. They transformed the path into a mosaic. Not the quality of a Gaudi perhaps but good enough to impress a small child.

Vintage china reminds me of a particularly happy summer when my children were young and I made friends with another mother who loved to give tea parties and bake cakes. She gathered her friends at the end of the school day and gave us afternoon tea. There was lots of pretty vintage china in evidence, lots of animated conversation and lots of laughter. Our children delved into her dressing up box and emerged as princesses in flowing robes or knights in shining armour. Sadly, my friend and her family moved on. They left the village taking their lovely children, dressing up boxes and vintage china with them.

Many years later, when my mother came to live with me, afternoon tea became part of my life again. We enjoyed afternoon tea together each day, in the garden when it was fine, indoors when it wasn't. I used pretty table cloths and vintage china and we sampled the delights of the cakes on offer in the locality. I've almost reached the age when afternoon tea would, once again, be a welcome addition to my day.

The bric-a-brac shelves in any charity shop are always worth a look. There is the faint possibility of finding valuable items but the certainty of finding interesting ones. If it's valuables you want, then look in the glass case because that's usually where they are kept. I don't often look because that's not why I'm there. I want the inexpensive and affordable items but occasionally I've looked and occasionally I've bought.

My glass case buys are very few but I have a manicure set, a pocket watch and a pink pearl necklace. All three were a fraction of the price they would have been. Have I discovered any extremely valuable treasure? Not yet, but am I satisfied with my purchases? Yes, I am.

This beautiful jewellery box, a triumph of
craftsmanship, made of wood inlaid with ebony and
mother of pearl, was found amongst the bric-a-brac in
a charity shop.

Bric-a-brac in a charity shop.

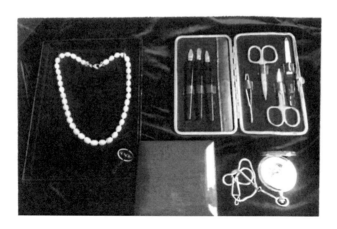

A glass case in a charity shop containing the more valuable items sold there.

Things I have bought from other glass cases.

Gold decoration on china, on the rim, round the edge or part of a pattern looks attractive but china with any gold decoration cannot be used in a microwave and probably not in a dishwasher. As a result, in recent years it has fallen out of favour and found its way to the charity shop often by way of the auction room.

A dinner service with gold rims and a few plates missing didn't sell at auction. I saw it in a charity shop. Did I buy it? Yes, I did; it was hand-painted in Hong Kong. I love it and got it for a very reasonable price. It shares a cupboard with four Royal Worcester dishes and five soufflé ramekins which also have gold decorations and were banished to a charity shop because of it.

A few years later, I found a dinner service abandoned on the floor of a charity shop. Why? Because it had thick, luxurious gold bands around its edge. Did I buy it? Yes, I did. I was delighted with it. It's perfect, new and complete and there's a lot of it. I have given it a cupboard all of its own. There are teacups included in it and they are a particularly attractive shape. I am reminded of the numerous drawing assignments I have set my art and design students involving cups. The ellipses are especially tricky to draw.

I have many examples of drawing and painting in my portfolio that were used to demonstrate particular points and give an idea of the excellent standard of work I was expecting to see. This is a photograph of a photocopy. It was a drawing assignment entitled 'A storm in a teacup' and a silver spoon was an optional extra.

My dinner service with its luxurious gold rings.
Crystal glasses collected from charity shops.

I used this drawing as an example of excellence.

The ellipses on the cups are difficult to draw. Thank you to the student who drew it.

This is a cup from my dinner service which is a similar shape.

Chairs were another of my frequently set drawing challenges and one of my chairs, another thrifty purchase, has been a temporary resident in several art departments and inspired some excellent work. I don't have any drawings of it but here is a photograph of a photocopy of another chair used to establish a standard for that assignment.

Proficient line drawing, followed by an understanding of tone was fundamental to the art and design course.

I was given a particularly impressive book of Leonardo Da Vinci's work when I was twenty-three and I used it throughout my teaching career to show how tone, when added to a line drawing, gives an impression of solidity, an illusion of the third dimension. My book has been into lots of schools and inspired many students.

I have always enjoyed reading and appreciated books. Space is limited but I do have a few books. The first book I bought was Chevreul on Colours and I still have it. I found it on a market stall and bought it for a few pounds. Years later, book clubs had their moment and I bought several books from them. It was only very recently that I realised what wonderful books are available in some charity shops. I am talking about large hardback 'coffee table' books which would normally be very expensive. Have I bought any? Yes, I have. They cost a few pounds and represent amazing value for money.

This chair belongs to me. It has been taken into many schools and drawn by many students.

I used this drawing of a chair as an example of excellence. Thank you that student.

Progressing from line drawings to tonal studies.
Leonardo da Vinci shows us how it's done.

If you are a brave and creative soul and have a house to furnish, go to Emmaus. I wasn't quite brave enough to buy the gold lacquered and gilded purple velvet dining room chairs I saw there – yes, I did say purple velvet! They definitely spoke to me and the artistic spirit that still miraculously survives within me yelled, "Buy them". I was tempted but common sense prevailed, it yelled even louder with a resounding, "Don't be an idiot!" Did I get them? No, I didn't. I was certainly tempted to buy the trees. A veritable forest of them arrived. Apparently, they had come from the foyer of a municipal building. Each tree was in a tub. The tubs were large and so were the trees. They were artificial but of good quality and looked amazing. They needed to be inside a large conservatory and unfortunately I don't have one. The mirror was bevelled glass with a gold ornate frame. It was gorgeous, really good quality and at a very reasonable price. Did I buy it? No, I didn't but I wished I had so I hurried back but it was gone.

Prices at Emmaus are very different to elsewhere. You will be very pleasantly surprised. There are lots of bargains to be found but you mustn't hesitate if you want it, buy it. They get the ordinary and the extraordinary. It's well worth a look.

Can I afford it? Sometimes, I can. Why can I afford it? Because I am careful with my money.

Can I afford to buy a large country house with orchards, extensive grounds and stables set on several acres of land? No, I can't, but I can afford membership of The National Trust so I can visit one.

'Coffee table' books for adults and also books for children – my grandchildren have been the lucky recipient of these.

I can step through the gates of historic houses, admire the fascinating artefacts and walk in the delightful grounds with orchards full of fruit and herbaceous borders full of exquisite plants. I can admire the creativity of the topiary, the perfume of the rose garden then emerge a few hours later and return to reality refreshed and rejuvenated by the experience.

My reality isn't luxurious but the area where I live is extremely beautiful and has lots to offer at very little cost. I can enjoy a day without spending vast amounts of money. I might do a bit of charity shop treasure hunting before progressing to a bit of window shopping. There is no expectation of being able to buy what I admire but it gives me pleasure and is absolutely free.

The quality of the window displays is crucial of course and because I live in close proximity to Stroud, Cirencester and Cheltenham, I am certain to see lots of 'well-dressed' windows. I have family living in Cheltenham so I go there quite often and, having enjoyed their company for a little while, I then wander off to window shop.

I love chandeliers and I know that a glance into the window of a chandelier shop is enough to lift my spirits.

My fascination with chandeliers began many years ago in a very unlikely place. I must have been about eleven or twelve when, once a week, I walked from my home to an area that was known as The Terraces. I still remember the sense of foreboding on the walk there and the relief on the walk back.

My trepidation was caused by my imminent piano lesson. Had I done enough practise? Probably not. I was about to find out. I waited in a tiny front room containing a piano and a large and impressive chandelier. Incongruous companions and yet each had transformative powers.

As I approached the terraced house, I sometimes heard the most sublimely beautiful piano music so I knew what that piano was capable of and sometimes as I waited for my lesson, a beam of light shone through the window of that drab room and the chandelier split it into a myriad of rainbows which danced over the walls and ceiling in a joyous outburst of colour.

My fascination with the mood-enhancing power of chandeliers began then and there. Did I ever succeed in creating sublimely beautiful sounds on the piano? No, I didn't, but my love of music began then and so those lessons were hugely influential and, of course, there was that delightful chandelier.

One of my favourite chandelier shops is to be found in the area known as The Suffolks in Cheltenham. It is huge and absolutely filled with chandeliers of all shapes and sizes. They are all made from crystal as they need to be if they are to create rainbows.

The Suffolks is a small and attractive part of Cheltenham filled with independent retailers. There are other chandeliers to admire there and several independently owned boutiques selling vintage and preowned designer clothes. It's perfect for window shopping, browsing and the very occasional purchase.

It is very close to Montpellier, another fascinating part of Cheltenham which has a chandelier shop and a delightful shop called Beatrice von Tresckow which lifts my spirits in the same way as a sunrise or sunset, a rainbow or a snowflake, all very different yet all very beautiful.

Chandelier shops. These are in the Suffolks area of Cheltenham.

Beatrice von Tresckow creates sophisticated shapes in luxurious fabrics. There are glowing colours and some intricate embroidery. The effect is stunning and at times theatrical. The prices reflect the quality of the workmanship and are beyond the purse of most people but the visual effect is fabulous and completely free.

Window shopping, I adore it – give it a go. You walk miles without realising it. Your senses are enlivened with a vast array of visual stimuli and you needn't spend a penny, it is completely free and hugely therapeutic.

A typical Saturday might consist of a charity shop treasure hunt followed by a bit of window shopping and finally food shopping, the most important task of the day.

I take food shopping very seriously. The food must be ethically sourced and of good quality, it must be fresh because if it is not, then many of its health-enhancing nutrients will have lost their potency. If possible, I like my food locally sourced and seasonal to reduce our carbon footprint.

If you live near a farm or a market garden, go and pick your own fruit and vegetables. They are fresher, they are cheaper and it's fun. Give it a try! Years ago, when I had more mouths to feed, I found buying directly from a farm cost-effective. I bought a large sack of potatoes, a box of Bramley cooking apples and any other bargains that they had an offer.

I look forward to the soft fruit season and listen for picking alerts to say when the fruit is ripe and ready. The farm I go to is convenient, it is also in a very pretty location and on a warm summer's day, with the sun shining, it's a real seasonal treat. Give it a try.

Preloved clothes shops in the Suffolks. One has now relocated.

Chandeliers in the Montpellier area of Cheltenham and a shop interior with a chandelier in it in the centre of Cheltenham. This shop has now relocated to London.

Bright and beautiful, a joy to behold!

I'm a very fussy food shopper wherever I'm buying. I like a bargain but I'm not prepared to compromise on quality. That said, I apply the same logic to food shopping as I do to my charity shop treasure hunt. If it's been a good growing season for cherries resulting in a glut of luscious cherries at a very reasonable price, I don't move them aside to get to a peach. I buy the cherries.

If our unpredictable English weather has given us a good season for plums and there they are, ripe, ready and reasonably priced, then I buy the plums. I make the most of the opportunity, I buy lots of plums. There will be plum crumble, possibly plum jam and most meals will be accompanied by plums for several days to come. They are good for your health and these ones will be good for your purse. What's not to like?

Next week, there will be other fruit on special offer. Buy perishable fruit and vegetables in season and hope for a good harvest. You know it makes sense. You have become a bargain hunter so put your shopping list aside. Food shopping has suddenly become more interesting although cooking has just become more challenging.

Not only can you bag a bargain at a charity shop, but market stalls selling fruit and vegetables sometimes have bargain bags too. The optimum time to arrive is half an hour before they close. They are determined to sell everything so unsold perishable produce is often put into bags, vegetable bags with a mix of vegetables or fruit bags with a mix of fruit. They are excellent value for money and make for some very creative cooking.

My first experience of market shopping began in Birmingham as a newly qualified teacher with a large appetite and very little money. I was new to the area and happened to discover a large Saturday market where unsold meat was auctioned at the end of the day. A large crowd gathered, each piece of meat was held up, offers were made and going, going, gone, it was sold to the highest bidder. Given the enthusiasm of the crowd, it was best to buy it first and examine it later. It was easy to tell if it was beef lamb or pork but should it be boiled, braised or roasted? Confronted with this uncertainty, casserole cooking was often the solution; it guaranteed delicious meals for very low prices and a minimum of effort.

Whilst I'm an enthusiastic food shopper, I'm a cautious cook. My first attempt at baking burst into flames and I've proceeded with caution ever since. Now I'm reasonably competent but I'm not a natural multi-tasker and so I usually opt for the fail-safe option. With savoury dishes, casseroles are still my personal favourite. Put everything in a casserole dish and leave it alone for a long time. I can do that! Eventually, a sort of alchemy occurs, wonderful smells waft around the kitchen and a delicious meal is ready to enjoy.

Some very impressive pans are appearing in charity shops at the moment. Why? Because of induction hobs. Thank you, induction hobs! Anyone who buys one has to buy a completely new set of pans which is exactly why I now have several new and impressive pans and am in the process of creating some new and equally impressive recipes. Happy days!

You may be blessed with children who choose to live in lovely locations. One of my sons set up a home in Surrey and I suddenly found that I had the opportunity to visit a whole range of new places. A season ticket gave me unlimited access to Kew Gardens which is spectacularly beautiful and an absolute delight. My particular favourite is the Palm House; step inside and you could be in the Amazonian jungle. Step outside and you realise that you are not. You are, in fact, conveniently near The Orangery which has delicious cakes and you may decide, very occasionally, to treat yourself to tea there.

London is a fascinating city and even better, many of its museums and galleries are absolutely free. The shops are also a delight. Liberty is one of my favourites, not because I wish to be liberated from anything in particular but because its interiors are so rich and sumptuous. Then there is Fortnum and Mason and Harrods to explore and wonderful window shopping opportunities to enjoy. After a few exhilarating and exhausting days there and having gathered a few memorable moments to brighten the occasional dull day, I'm happy to come home to my own world again.

Seeing the Christmas lights in London was a memorable experience. They were a visual delight, especially the angel lights, so very beautiful, shimmering with a delicate, ephemeral quality, truly breath-taking! They swayed gracefully on the breeze and seemed to be as fine and delicate as gossamer, they were a fabulous sight.

The whole city was transformed each evening by a myriad of lights. They seemed to be everywhere; in trees and windows, reflected in wet pavements or dancing on icy and snowy surfaces. Everything was bathed in a magical, shimmering glow, transformative, theatrical, mesmerising and absolutely free. I was able to wander around, transported by the scene, enjoying the uplifting extravaganza that is Christmas in London.

Kew Gardens – I absolutely love Kew Gardens

Cotswold Christmases are also splendid affairs, traditional age-honoured customs perfected over time. Each town and village is dressed to impress in all its finery with street markets, sometimes an outdoor ice rink and an evening of celebration to mark the start of the festivities when the street lights and the Christmas tree lights are turned on.

Creative minds bring new ideas and one successful innovation, a new tradition in the making, started in one town and has spread to many more. It uses Christmas trees and a forest of them, beautifully lit and appropriately decorated, are gathered together each Christmas in the church. The trees publicise the clubs, societies, special interest groups, all the many social activities and opportunities available in the area. Each tree is decorated by its members to represent the society it is promoting and information about it and how to join is placed at its foot. Visitors are welcomed with music and refreshments and the age-old spirit of generosity and fellowship which is the spirit of Christmas, is created again. Do I go to admire them? Yes, of course I do and here are some of the photographs, don't they look amazing?

Each year, I dress our Christmas tree as part of those Christmas traditions. I bought our artificial tree in 1977. I took it home, saw that the hole in its trunk wasn't central and realised that it would lean to one side which it did and has done every year since. I have accepted and embraced this characterful quality and each Christmas I decide which way it will lean, to the right or to the left. When dressed in its finery, it looks beautiful.

Christmas Time in Cirencester. One of the many shops
selling gorgeous gifts and looking lovely

Christmas Tree festivals – a new tradition in the making

A few years ago, as Christmas approached, tree decorations flooded into the charity shops. These were large, magnificent, opulent. Did I buy some? Yes, I certainly did, I bought large gold ones in a variety of bold shapes, each with a raised embossed surface. I also bought apples and pears which glowed and glimmered. Finally, I bought some gold birds. I added my new tree decorations to my old ones and when my tree was dressed in its Christmas finery, it looked more beautiful than ever.

My house is furnished, my wardrobe drawers and cupboards are full. Have most of my possessions come from charity shops? Yes, they have. Is that obvious? No, it isn't. I owe a debt of gratitude to our charity shops. They have provided me with necessities and some luxuries. Thank you. It has been a pleasure, a rewarding and fascinating journey of discovery. I hope that I have encouraged others to value and enjoy what our charity shops have to offer. They are all different with their own unique personality. I urge you to go and explore them. I know that you won't be disappointed.

Has the charity shop been surpassed by people buying pre-loved and vintage clothing online?

I did wonder if that might happen but, in my mind, there is no contest. I know from experience that prospective purchases need to be subjected to close scrutiny, the kind that needs to be done up close and personal. If it's an article of clothing, it needs to be held up to artificial light, then examined in daylight, and then turned inside out. The label needs to be looked at, if it has one, and the quality of the fabric ascertained. The cut and the fit need to be considered and I hope that very soon, the chance to 'try before you buy' is reinstated. To buy or not to buy is always an agonising decision. I don't part with my money easily.

Large embossed Christmas Tree decorations

More Christmas Tree decorations

Think of all the admin involved in buying online and then having to package it up and return it if you decide that you don't like it. Think of the miles involved. The pleasure of the purchase would be seriously diminished for me and being the fussy person that I am, the admin would be colossal. Why make life difficult? Don't do it! Go to the charity shops instead.

I am a staunch supporter of charity shops. They have cheered me up on so many occasions when I felt disheartened, proved to me time after time that we all have a guardian angel watching over us and prevented me from sinking into a slurry of despond or some equally awful place.

There were very few Saturdays when I didn't pounce on a purchase and whilst it might be difficult to imagine that a potato peeler could actually lift your spirits, believe me, it can. The house proud but financially challenged person might find a super dooper potato peeler very desirable. It may not be in the same league as a spiraliser but it's a kitchen essential and could be considered a very lucky find!

This is not a book of collected and curated iconic fashion. I am not a fashionista. This is a financial survival guide.

I have chosen furnishings and clothing appropriate to my modest lifestyle. Classic, good quality in preference to fashionable every time. Paying the mortgage and giving my children nutritious food were my priorities. Another essential was a car to get to work to earn the money to do that. Surviving financially on a very small salary was not always easy.

We all make instant and superficial judgements about other people, this is a fact and as a young professional I tried to hide my 'economies'. I tried to merge in rather than stand out and only later as my expertise and funds increased did I buy anything that wasn't absolutely necessary.

I couldn't exceed my very limited budget so there were many occasions when I had to walk away from what I knew to be a genuine bargain and however loudly my inner diva yelled 'Get it', I listened to the more sensible me saying 'Put it back, put it back right now.' As a result, I missed some amazing bargains but I now own my own small house, my children were well-fed and are now healthy and successful adults. I have an old but serviceable car and I survived a long career in teaching so I do feel very loyal to the charity shops that have entertained and helped me.

Have I persuaded you? Are you a charity shop convert? Are you ready to reject the mindset of the fashionista, a slavish follower of fashion, in favour of eco-warrior credentials? If you do, you will be leading instead of following fashion, creating your own personal unique fashion statements and adopting a more sustainable lifestyle. You will be making better use of the planet's resources, not wasting what we have but recycling, upcycling, altering, adapting and reusing. You will be saving considerable amounts of money but you will also be helping the charities to help those in even greater need than you.

So many advantages resulting from one simple decision; to change how you shop. Will you do it? I hope you will.

Don't want to change your lifestyle? Don't want to change the way you shop? Then perhaps you could plant a tree. Even better, plant several trees. If everyone plants at least one tree, it will help heal the world that we are damaging by offsetting carbon emissions. Any kind of tree, although a fruit tree would be a very practical choice. Do it, do it for the next generation, do it today.

Then, of course, we have carbon sequestration to consider. 'Do we?' I hear you say. Yes, we do, because apparently, traditional wildflower meadows have mycorrhizal fungi which are even better 'carbon sinks' than woodland so we must do all we can to rewild the countryside and increase biodiversity.

In 2014, *The Farmers' Weekly* announced that there were only a hundred harvests left because intensive farming has damaged the quality of our soil. HELP! Thank you, The Painswick Conservation Group for that information; even if it did give me several sleepless nights, it was something I needed to know.

Can you help? Yes, you can. Should you help? Yes, in my opinion you very definitely should. Making small changes to the way we live our lives would make a huge difference. We have damaged our planet and it is our responsibility to try to heal it. We have a duty of care to the living creatures that inhabit the planet but we also have a duty of care to the planet itself. Make those small changes now, do it, do it today!

I know about trees and have already planted three fruit trees. I didn't know about the importance of rewilding but now I do and I will sow some wildflower seeds in my small garden. I'm not going to become a vegetarian, a vegan or a pescatarian any time soon but I will eat less meat. I like the occasional holiday abroad but I will have more staycations and I will continue to champion our charity shops.

Will my lifestyle changes help? I do hope so.

Some rewilding going on in the local allotments.
Don't the wildflowers look beautiful!

We are just emerging from a global pandemic only to be confronted by global warming. If you are finding life particularly challenging, then I hope that some of my strategies help.

I set off on lots of treasure hunts but did I ever find any treasure? Yes, I did.

As well as my purchases and the objets d'art that I inherited, I have a treasure chest full of memories. Some of them I've shared with you. When I feel discouraged or downhearted, I lift the lid and choose a happy memory. They are my own personal podcasts and the experiences of laughter and friendship that I once enjoyed are there to be enjoyed again and again and again. They are there whenever I need them.

Make some happy memories of your own, do it, do it today. Make as many happy memories as you can in what is still a spectacularly beautiful world.